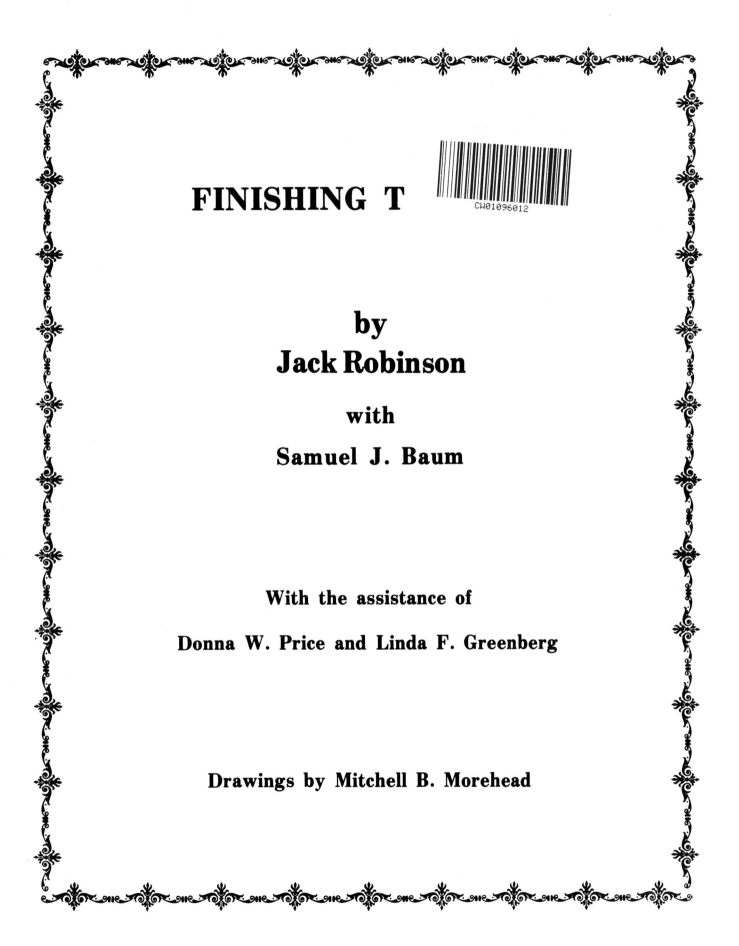

FINISHING T

by
Jack Robinson

with

Samuel J. Baum

With the assistance of

Donna W. Price and Linda F. Greenberg

Drawings by Mitchell B. Morehead

Greenberg Publishing Company, Inc.
7566 Main Street
Sykesville, Maryland 21784
(410) 795-7447

First Edition
Third Printing

Manufactured in the United States of America

Greenberg Publishing Company, Inc., publishes the world's largest selection of Lionel, American Flyer, LGB, Marx, Ives, and other toy train publications as well as a selection of books on model and prototype railroading, dollhouse building, and collectible toys. For a complete listing of current Greenberg publications, please call 1-800-533-6644 or write to Kalmbach Publishing, 21027 Crossroads Circle, Waukesha, Wisconsin 53187.

Greenberg Shows, Inc., sponsors *Greenberg's Great Train, Dollhouse and Toy Shows*, the world's largest of their kind. The shows feature extravagant operating train layouts and a display of magnificent dollhouses. The shows also present a huge marketplace of model and toy trains, for HO, N, and Z Scales; Lionel O and Standard Gauges; S, and 1 Gauges; plus layout accessories and railroadiana. They also offer a large selection of dollhouse miniatures and building materials, and collectible toys. Shows are scheduled along the East Coast each year from Massachusetts to Florida. For a list of our current shows, please call (410) 795-7447 or write to Greenberg Shows, Inc., 7566 Main Street, Sykesville, Maryland 21784 and request a show brochure.

Greenberg Auctions, a division of Greenberg Shows, Inc., offers nationally advertised auctions of toy trains and toys. Please contact our auction manager at (410) 795-7447 for further information.

ISBN 0-89778-045-0

Library of Congress Cataloging-in-Publication Data

Robinson, Jack   1943
    Finishing Touches.

      1. Doll-houses.   2. Doll Furniture   I. Baum, Samuel J. II. Title.
TT175.3.R63 1986   745.592-3   89-29531
ISBN 0-89778-045-0

Table of Contents

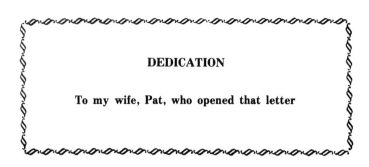

DEDICATION

To my wife, Pat, who opened that letter

Acknowledgments

Jack Robinson, a patient and persevering man, is a very creative miniaturist and master builder. And *FINISHING TOUCHES* is a book that was "a-building" for many months. It grew from the ideas, concepts and drawings provided by Jack, from the photographs taken by George Stern and Tim Parrish, and from the initial editings by Donna Price and myself. But, the book really came together with the guidance of Samuel Baum who, with Jack, crafted a well-rounded yet exacting how-to-build-it guide.

Mitchell Morehead, an interior design instructor at The International Institute of Interior Design in Washington, D.C. provided the handsome line drawings which help to elucidate the four chapters. Donna Price, graphics artist, helped organize and arrange the book.

Jack is planning to write several other books in this dollhouse series. Please write to him, in care of Greenberg Publishing, to let us know what finishing projects you would next like him to undertake.

Linda Greenberg
Publisher
October 16, 1986

Introduction
THE HOUSE THAT JACK BUILT

Take four rectangular pieces of wood and tack them together to form a kind of box. Take two more pieces, nail them together at a 45 degree angle and set them on top as a cover. Cut a few square and rectangular holes at strategic places in the sides and what you have looks vaguely like a house...but, it's not.

Houses have shingles on the roof and stone at the foundation. They have hardy chimneys of brick climbing the sides, and windows outlined with shutters and blossoming window boxes. Inside, the floors are oak and the walls are papered to create a feeling of congeniality and warmth. In short, it is the presence of these things, the *FINISHING TOUCHES*, which makes four walls and a roof into a home.

My name is Jack Robinson and I've been designing and building dollhouses for 10 years. I was first introduced to the charm of the miniature world by my Grandmother when I was a boy. She gave me a tiny lantern, an exact duplicate of its prototype, but somehow more magical for its delicate size. It seemed almost as if it should be carried in the diminutive fist of some mythological creature, perhaps a leprechaun searching for gold in the dead of night.

That was the beginning, and I still, to this day, have the lantern. After receiving that treasure, everything had to be miniature. Miniature pots and pans, and miniature glass urns. There was even a tiny harmonica that really worked. And I carefully displayed them, laid out on shelves for all to admire.

But, it was years later that my interest in dollhouses was sparked. I was doing a little work at some friends' house one day (I am also a renovator of older homes and fire damaged buildings; the homes I have renovated have ranged from the Modern to the Victorian to the pre-Civil War period) and I saw them struggling to build a dollhouse from a kit. Now, I'd been into miniatures for a long time and had never gotten involved with dollhouses, but it struck me that with my background, I should be able to easily build one from scratch.

That evening, on the way home, I designed, cut and constructed an entire house in my head. The next day, I gathered the materials and did it for real.

It was crude, but it was a beginning and I quickly saw what needed to be done to give it life. During the following week or so, I practiced my technique and built several more dollhouses. I carted them down to a local dollhouse and miniatures shop where they were displayed for sale. Lo and behold, they quickly sold out and special orders for more were placed. The rest, as they say, is history.

I embarked on this how-to-build-it series not so much from my need to become an author, but to answer the many people who have asked me how they can fix-up or redesign their dollhouses. Though for me, building dollhouses is a business, I come to it from the same perspective as any hobbyist. The time that I spend designing and constructing a house, delving into even the smallest details, is a relaxing, quiet time, and the kind words that I hear from those who admire my work are very rewarding.

And it is for those people, who so often have asked me how I achieve such a uniquely realistic look, that I write this book. It is my intention, as each volume develops, to reveal my personal techniques for dollhouse building. They are tried and true methods, and I believe them to be, in many cases, superior to those which often accompany pre-fab kits and component pieces. They also give the added benefit of being readily adaptable to your own personal dollhouse designs, thus freeing you from the constraints of having to construct someone else's dreams.

It is true that all dollhouses are not the same. However, there are basic building procedures which allow the information in this series to apply almost universally. The vast majority of dollhouses are built on a one-inch-to-the-foot scale. Any measurements which I give are based on that scale. If you are building a house on, say, a half-inch-to-the-foot scale, you will have to adjust the plans accordingly.

I encourage you to do more than follow my instructions, ending up with a duplicate of my samples. It is impossible to show, for example, every style of chimney that one could make, so simply use my diagrams as a guide to laying out your designs.

In the *FINISHING TOUCHES* series, I will delve into a wide range of dollhouse topics. This book, Volume I, focuses on how to create an innovative lightweight, realistic brick out of wooden coffee stirrers; how to build a solid foundation with a real concrete block look; how to lay actual wood plank floors which would be a delight to have even in a real home; and how to cut simple but effective trimming to authenticate any dollhouse interior.

Future volumes will introduce more intricate projects and teach you how to handle your tools with greater skill so that the unusual cuts which the jobs require can be executed with ease.

Besides actual finishing, I will also describe how to build add-on pieces for your miniature scenes. For example, how to build tiny orange crates to serve as stylish shelves in a child's room, or a beautifully-trellised gazebo for a garden scene. On a slightly larger scale, I will teach you how to build a down-to-earth miniature treehouse using a real tree limb. It looks great in a rustic woods setting.

The world of dollhouses and miniatures is truly an enchanting place. It is easy to enter, and once you are there, it gives you the freedom to design and build it as you please.

If I were to give you any extra advice it would be this...relax and enjoy yourself. There is no project so difficult that even a novice couldn't accomplish it with time. So be patient. Rome wasn't built in a day...not even in miniature.

Chapter 1
BRICK IS BACK

Constructing a realistic, substantial brick home is the ideal of many dollhouse builders. But, whether one is looking to build an all-brick dwelling or more typically desires only an ornamental brick fireplace, chimney or window/doorway trim, the problems most often encountered derive from the ready-made miniature bricks which are heavy and awkward to work with. Challenged by this problem, I have developed what I consider to be a realistic brick very suitable for dollhouse walls, chimneys and floors that is lightweight and easy to manipulate in small pieces. It is inexpensive as well.

Figure 1-1 Compare the two buildings. On the left is an historic house located in Fredericksburg, Virginia. On the right is my replica of it, scaled one-inch-to-the-foot. I decided to build it because I enjoyed the original's rustic chimney so much. Its 1,274 simulated bricks were made from coffee stirrers.

As a bricklayer, you will have to devote some time and patience to the project, however my instructions are easy to understand and follow, and even an experienced craftsperson will pick up many useful tips. It is important to remember to carefully read and follow the instructions on any product purchased, although on occasion I recommend my own techniques as well. Also, as we all know, "Beauty is in the eye of the beholder." Consider the effect you wish to accomplish and what approach will best help you to achieve it. There may be times when my instructions should be modified to meet individual requirements. In fact, any time a new wrinkle or method for handling one of my techniques is found, please let me know so that we can share it with our other readers.

I have always had a fascination for chimneys. They give a house a firm, well-rooted feeling and impart a certain geniality that is lacking in many of the tract homes constructed today. For that reason the chimney is my focus for this bricklaying project. In

Part I, I explain how to construct its frame, and in Part II, go on to describe how to lay the bricks.

When you reach the bricking section, keep in mind that the techniques for laying bricks on a chimney are generally the same as would apply to laying bricks on almost any surface, such as an exterior wall or fireplace. I demonstrate this by rounding off the chapter with some hints on how to lay a brick floor or walkway.

PART I — CONSTRUCTING A CHIMNEY FRAME

The first thing you will need to do is decide on the type and placement of the chimney or chimneys on your house. While one chimney certainly adds a nice touch to almost any home, if you are duplicating a large, older period house you may want to consider the possibility of having two chimneys, one on each end. Also consider the chimneys in light of the logical placement of the fireplaces within the house. Many older mansions had fireplaces in the inner rooms and/or on the second floor, in which case you may want to construct a chimney stack or two along the roof, as well as the main ones on the sides.

Should you have trouble in coming up with an appropriate chimney for your house, there are several magazines on the market to which you could refer. The photographs in *Southern Living* and *Better Homes and Gardens*, in particular, always seem to capture the entire house with a good view of the chimney.

Because there are many styles and sizes of dollhouses, not to mention kits and custom-built houses, what I give you here are instructions for building a very basic chimney. You will need to make some adjustments for your house and for the type of chimney which you wish to create. If pictures to which you can refer are not available, do some drawings to help you visualize the project better.

Materials and Tools

Plywood 1/4"—a scrap piece of wall paneling will do
Pine strips 1/2" x 3/4"—can be purchased at a hardware or lumber store; sometimes referred to as "stop molding"
Wood glue
Sandpaper—medium grit
C-clamps or a heavy weight or 3/4" brads
Saber saw
Pencil
Ruler
Hammer (if using brads; read text first)

To Work!

Start out by drawing the front of your chimney design on a piece of cardboard. It should be life-size, in scale with your dollhouse. Make sure it reaches 2" to 3" above the roof; in this way the chimney will comply, in scale, with the national fire code, which sets their height regulations with the thought that should any sparks go up the flue, they will fall to the side or burn up as they travel skyward, and the roof will not catch fire.

If technical details are important to you, and you are unsure about the authenticity of your chimney, check out some architectural design books at the local library. They will give specific drawings and details, and will tell you the regular building standards for chimneys including foundations, sizes and flues. Of course, if these details do not interest you, go with my number one rule: What looks good to the eye is what is good for the house.

Cut out your drawing and trace its outline on the plywood, then use the saber saw to cut the design out of the wood.

The chimney sides are made from 1/2" x 3/4" pine strips. If your local hardware store does not have the strips, they can be cut from a 3/4" board on a table top saw. Many lumberyards or building supply stores are willing to do the job for a small fee.

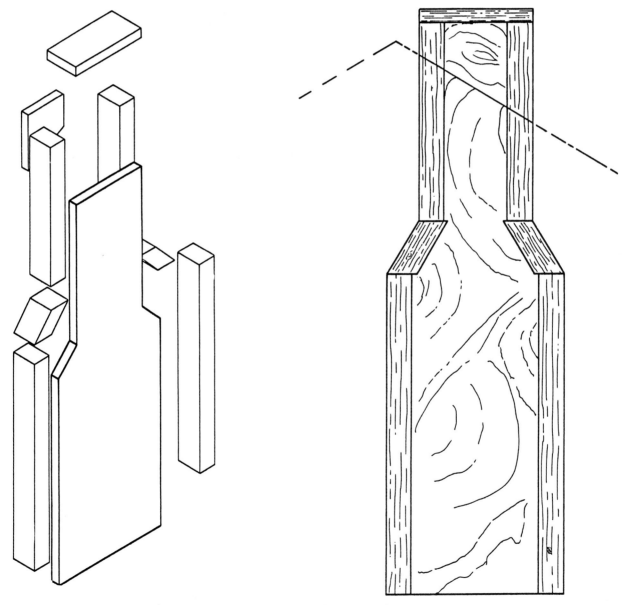

Figure 1-2   On the left is an exploded diagram of a simple chimney frame. To the right is a cutaway of the same frame.

9

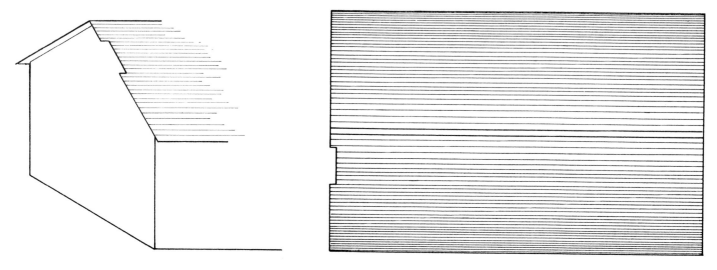

Figure 1-3 A roof with a notch cut out for the chimney.

Figure 1-2 shows how to construct a simple chimney which tapers into a narrow upper section. Each side is made from three strips of wood, two vertical and one on an angle. Cut and glue the long upper and lower vertical strips first since these have square cut edges. Then cut the angled strips to size—a hint: if you cut them a smidgen too long, it will be simple to sand down the edges for a tight fit. Glue on the angled strips.

Use C-clamps, a heavy weight, or hammer in 3/4" brads to hold the plywood and pine strips tightly together.

The fourth side of the chimney, the inner side which shows only above the roof, is indicated in Figure 1-2. Hold your drawing of the chimney against the dollhouse and mark it where it meets the roof. Cut out the piece and use it as a template for cutting the fourth side from the plywood. Glue the plywood piece onto the chimney.

Close off the top of the chimney also with a piece of plywood. Lay a small scrap on the top and draw a line on it going around the chimney. Cut out the piece out and glue it in place.

With the chimney completed, place it next to the house. If your house has a slight roof overhang, or maybe a few wood shingles over the edge, cut out a notch with a knife or X-acto saw (see Figure 1-3) so that the chimney will sit firmly against the side of the dollhouse. Once the fit is good, glue the chimney in place.

Though you could simply paint the chimney the same color as the dollhouse and leave it at that, I would heartily recommend that you finish a good job properly and cover it with brick. Continue on and I will show you a way to finish your chimney so realistically that the only way one could tell it is not the real thing is by its size.

PART II – BRICKING A CHIMNEY

At this point the chimney frame is built and attached to the house, and now you are ready to get into the glamour part of the job—bricking the chimney. Though it is somewhat time consuming, it is also most rewarding to see a bare frame gradually turn into real chimney. (And the compliments which you are sure to garner are just as rewarding!)

When designing your chimney, you should take into account more than just the chimney's overall structure—the brickwork, too, should conform to the house style. If yours is a Colonial house with clean lines, then you want the brickwork to be just as true and sharp; if you have built a cottage in the country, then you may prefer a more rustic look. If copying the brickwork of a real chimney, know exactly how it appears. A detailed drawing which shows the exact brick layout would help.

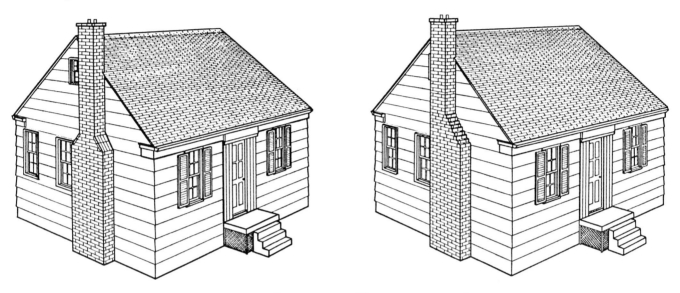

Figure 1-4 Four common chimney arrangements.

Most miniature bricklayers do, in fact, endeavor to duplicate the look and feel of a specific brick chimney or facade. Therefore, the choice of brick color and finish are as critical as is the overall structure.

If striving to achieve a traditional look, boxcar red will, in most cases, be an excellent exterior color. It is not bright or flashy, but has a pleasing intensity. Though most hobby shops carry many appropriately brick-looking shades of red/red-orange, etc., you may wish to duplicate a brighter color, for example a bright orange-red as may be found on today's newer homes. In this case, the color will have to be mixed. It is easy to do, but will take some time and patience while experimenting to get just the right shade. It may be helpful to ask the advice of a more experienced person in a paint or hardware store.

It is also not unusual to paint the brick and mortar the same color as the house. In fact, in canvassing the houses in any neighborhood one might find that many have brick and mortar matching the exterior finish.

If doing any interior brickwork, for example a fireplace, boxcar red may not be as good a choice. It is a subdued color and in a small and perhaps not well-lit room the fireplace will fade into the shadows and not do justice to the piece. In this case it would be better to use a lighter or brighter red that will make the brickwork stand out for all to admire. On the other hand, because boxcar red bricks do blend into most settings, they can lend a room a cordial, earthy feeling.

Materials and Tools

Expect that supplies will cost between $10 and $15 unless the tools and materials are on hand. This, of course, will vary according to the amount of area to be bricked. Most items can be purchased at hobby and/or hardware stores. Any tools bought will also be useful in doing other types of miniature work, however read the instructions before making any purchases.

Jig (the builder will make as explained below)
X-acto fine-tooth saw
X-acto miter box
Small C-clamp
Wood glue—used for gluing wood or paper to like substances
Tweezers
Pencil
Ruler
Fine and medium grit sandpaper
Razor blade or sharp knife
Scrap wood
Joint compound (either a dry or premixed compound)
Paint (probably boxcar red, but see discussion of paints below before making purchase)
Wooden coffee stirrers

More About Stirrers

The wooden coffee stirrers are the most important component of this project, as your bricks will be made from them. I recommend the round-ended type (see Figure 1-5).

They are very uniform in size, and measure 5-1/2 inches long by 1/4 of an inch wide by 1/16th of an inch thick. They are often found in convenience stores and fast food restaurants, and most store managers will strike a deal and sell a box for about $1. You might also try a local restaurant supply wholesaler.

The advantage of my wooden coffee stirrer "bricks" is that they are lightweight and inexpensive. Pre-fabricated bricks are heavy, as are real bricks, and they are relatively expensive to buy in quantity.

Figure 1-5　An actual size coffee stirrer used for making bricks.

In addition, an X-acto fine-tooth saw and a miter box will be needed to cut the stirrers. Both are found in many small workshops. They involve the greatest expense — about $10 for both.

Figure 1-6　A Jig is essential for most woodworking or brickmaking. After the jig is set, it will hold the work precisely in position so that when cutting out bricks, each one will be the same size.

Preparing the Bricks

The first tool listed, a jig, is essential for most woodworking or brickmaking. Its purpose is to hold the wood precisely in position so that, in this case, when cutting out bricks, each one will be of a uniform size.

Place the miter box on a work table and construct the jig by clamping a squared-off piece of scrap wood to it as shown in Figure 1-6. This simple jig may be slid along the miter box so that when the wood is butt up against it, any length can be quickly and cleanly cut. It would be a good idea to practice cutting a few sample "bricks" of between 1/2 and 5/8 of an inch long just to get a feel for the work, and having a variety of lengths for comparison helps to determine the size brick best suited to your particular project.

Figure 1-7 Detail of a simple chimney.

To choose your brick size, plan on laying the first row of bricks so that you start with a full-sized brick on one side and continue across so that you end with a full-sized brick (see Figure 1-7). Conversely, on the second row, you will start with a "butt", or half-sized brick, and continue laying bricks to end with a butt brick. Obviously, then, the size of your bricks is partly determined by the number needed to begin and end the rows evenly.

Having chosen a suitable size, cut several sample bricks and lay them on the chimney (or surface to be bricked over) to check the fit. (Note: It is not necessary to cut any half-size bricks for this project, as will be explained.) There should be about 1/8 to 1/16 of an inch of space between each brick for the mortar. This can vary a little and not diminish the effect of the work, but it is best to be careful in advance when planning out each course—you want to avoid reaching the top of the chimney and finding that you have to cut the last row of bricks lengthwise in order to get them to fit.

After all the bricks are cut out, the next step is to draw horizontal lines with a pencil on the chimney, from the bottom to the top, spacing each line about 3/8 of an inch apart. The lines will show where to place the bricks so that they are laid straight. Having the bricks in uniform rows gives a chimney a sharp, clean look.

Now, starting with the bottom of the front side of the chimney, put a few drops of wood glue on the bricks and lay them in place. Work from the bottom up and remember that the first row should begin and end on full-size bricks. When you lay the rows beginning and ending on half-bricks, glue the full-size brick on so that half of it hangs over the edge (see Figure 1-8). The excess will be cut off later.

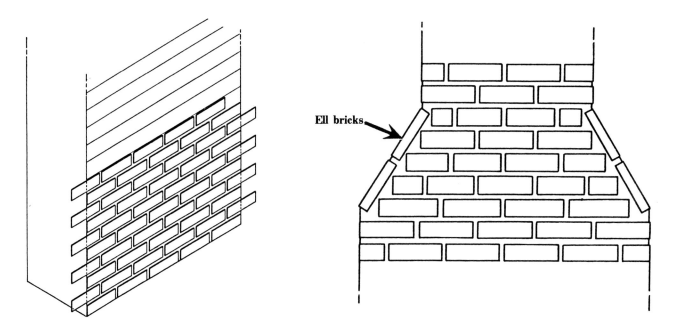

Figure 1-8 Detail showing overhanging bricks. The excess brick should be cut off after the glue has dried.

Figure 1-9 Front view detail of the tapered section of a chimney.

When the section of the chimney that tapers in is reached, shift the bricks a little so that you fill in only the middle section. These bricks should not hang over and room should be left for the slanted ell bricks as shown in Figure 1-9. The ell bricks are made from full size bricks cut in half length-wise.

Cover the upper narrow section of the chimney above the taper in the same manner as was done on the lower part, with alternating rows starting and ending with full or butt bricks.

After the glue has completely dried (it usually takes 30 to 45 minutes), take the X-acto fine tooth saw and carefully trim off the overhanging bricks. Lightly sand the rough edges with a piece of medium grit sandpaper so that they are completely flush with the chimney sides. Sometimes a few splinters will come off during the sanding. Do not try to glue them back on unless they are really big.

Next, go on to the sides of the chimney and repeat the above process. Remember, it is very important to coordinate the side rows with the front rows—a full-size brick on the front edge should meet a butt brick on the side in order to give the illusion of them being only one brick.

It may be necessary to recut a few bricks or to shift them somewhat between butt joints in order to line up those bricks which meet the back of the dollhouse. Or, as I have done, use a slightly different size brick on the sides than was used on the front. In any case, it is easy to recut or manipulate the bricks so as to achieve the desired affect.

On the tapered section of the chimney sides, line up all the bricks vertically, as shown in Figure 1-10. The detail drawing shows how the pieces on the tapered section should meet in order to form a single brick.

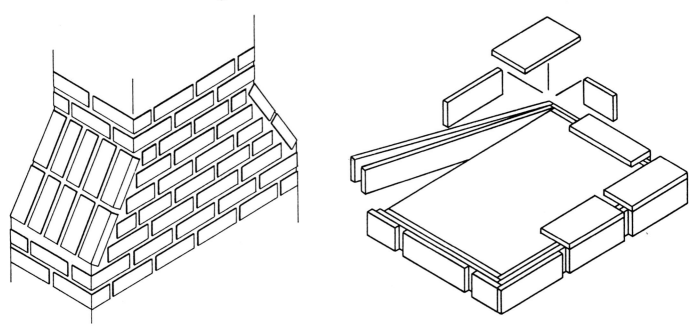

Figure 1-10   3/4 view detail of the tapered section of a chimney. Note the ell cap arrangement.

Figure 1-11   An exploded view of a chimney crown.

As the work progresses, and row-after-row the bricks begin to advance up the chimney, the masonry will begin to take on a realistic look. When each side is completed, let the glue thoroughly dry and then cut off the overhanging pieces. If the chimney has an exposed fourth side above the roof level, this should also be covered.

After all the sides are completed and sanded so that the edges are squarely aligned, slightly round the edges ever so gently with fine grit sandpaper.

The chimney top can be left as is, straight, or can be finished off with a crown. The crown can be made by laying down several layers of flat wood stock and then gluing bricks over top (see Figure 1-11). Remember to lay the pieces on the edges so that they appear to be one brick.

Another realistic addition would be a flue pipe. Cut the pipe from a dowel rod or square wood stock and glue it on top of the chimney. The surrounding space will be filled in with mortar.

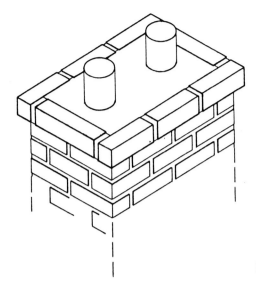

Figure 1-12 Flue pipes add realism to a chimney.

Finishing the Chimney

To finish the chimney decide whether you prefer the mortar to show or whether a more solidly brick appearance would be most appropriate.

If the mortar joints are to be more prominent, first paint the bricks in the chosen color. Again, I like a traditional boxcar red in a flat finish. Paint the entire brick surface. It does not matter if a little paint gets into the mortar joints or cracks because the mortar will be applied after the paint dries. Latex paint dries rather quickly, while it takes four to eight hours for an oil base paint to dry. Latex paint is also easier to use in terms of cleanup or correcting mistakes, but some people still prefer oil paints. Which ever type you chose, be sure to thoroughly read the manufacturer's application instructions before beginning. They will also state drying time and cleanup procedure.

Once the paint has dried, take a little joint compound and carefully rub it into all the joints or cracks between the bricks. Joint compound is water-based and should any get smeared on the bricks, it is easily wiped off with a damp cloth.

Should you wish to tint the joint compound, mix in a little food coloring. Proceed slowly and try out a few samples on a test board before applying it to the chimney. The colors tend to flatten out as the compound dries, so let it dry completely before passing judgement.

While working the compound in, run your finger or a nail along the joints to slightly indent them. This will add even more realism to the chimney's appearance. Completely cover the entire chimney wherever there are bricks. If you have put in flue pipes, completely surround them with the compound.

As the compound is applied and the excess wiped off, a real transformation will take place, as a wall of little pieces of wood becomes a miniature life-like chimney. If some cracking in the mortar occurs, do not be upset, this is normal. Joint compound tends to shrink as it dries. Just apply more of the compound and wipe it smooth.

If the mortar is not to show prominently, apply the joint compound first; then paint over the entire chimney only after the compound has thoroughly dried.

Finally, there are a couple ways to realistically "age" a chimney. Take a small piece of charcoal and gently blacken the chimney's top and about two inches of each side so that it takes on a sooty and used appearance. Do not uniformly blacken the sides or top, but use your fingers to rub in streaks and different gradations of soot.

Figure 1-13 A chimney can be painted in two different styles.

Bricks painted first, then mortar applied.

Mortar applied, then the entire surface painted.

Another way to "age" a chimney is to use a nail to gently scratch a few joints at various places. This will immitate the cracking affect that cold or thawing weather has on real brick and mortar.

As you get into the job, I think you will find that laying bricks is fun and simple to do. Whether making a chimney, a fireplace, or just a wall, the most important thing is to plan the entire project out completely. Examine the real-life prototypes and make drawings.

Although here I have described how to build a rather conventional chimney with uniform bricks, you will find that a little imagination goes a long way. By adapting my methods and cutting different sizes of bricks or using a variety of colors, you should have no problem in designing your own realistic brick job. Take your time and enjoy yourself.

Figure 1-14 With charcoal rubbed in, the chimney takes on a used look.

PART III — FLOORS, WALKWAYS AND PATIOS

I have decided to include this epilogue in order to demonstrate how easy it is to adapt my bricking techniques to other projects. The tools and materials are essentially the same as used above and, as always, you will find that most of the hard work revolves around the planning, not the doing.

To cover a kitchen floor or a walkway such as an outside sidewalk there are a few added steps when arranging the bricks. First, determine the layout pattern which is most compatible with the space and feeling of your dollhouse. Some examples of common sidewalk brick patterns are presented below in Figure 1-15.

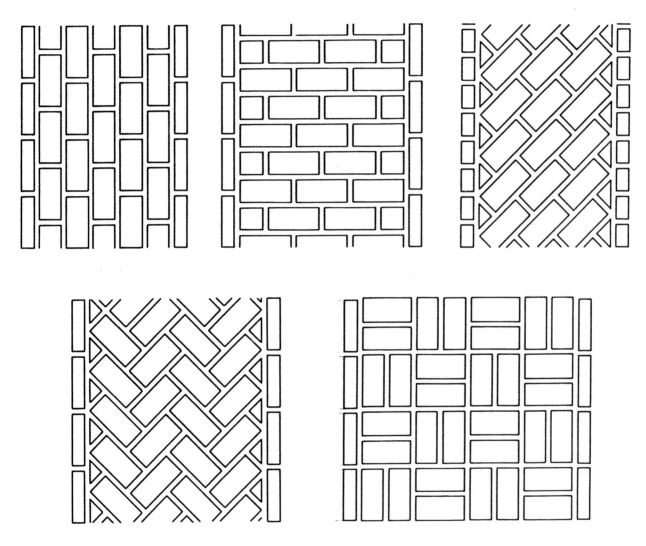

Figure 1-15   Five common paving patterns.

Next, mark off lines on the surface to be covered to act as a guide for the placement of the bricks. A good way to layout some of the more complicated patterns would be to actually make a template by taking a couple of wooden stirrers and laying them across one another. Then it will be a simple matter of marking the pattern that their crossing makes.

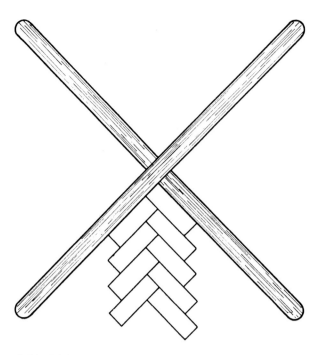

Figure 1-16 Make a template by crisscrossing two coffee stirrers.

For example, if you crisscross the sticks at a 45 degree angle, you can draw in the attractive basketweave or herringbone patterns so that they come out evenly (see Figure 1-16).

After the pattern has been adjusted so that it is as even as possible, check it by cutting a few sample bricks and laying them out. Do not forget to leave a slight space for mortar between the bricks. Use the samples to set up the jig for the proper length and cut out the rest of your bricks.

Of the designs shown, the hardest to make for beginners is the herringbone pattern. It requires very thorough planning of each brick's position in relation to the next. However, the pleasing results of this very quaint design are worth the effort.

The bricks are individually applied with wood glue in the same manner as bricks on a chimney or house foundation. Once the glue has dried, finish off the bricks by sanding them with a medium grade sandpaper. This will roughen up the surface and give it the proper texture of bricks that have been subjected to wear and tear from years of feet walking on them.

Paint the bricks in a color which best suits your project. However, for an authentic appearance, it's no surprise that I recommend a flat boxcar red.

Lastly, fill in the spaces between bricks with joint compound, as explained in the chimney section. For an inside brick floor, you may wish to fill in the spaces between the bricks first, and then paint over the entire floor. The brick color and finish are for the builder to decide. Do not forget that a somewhat brighter red will stand out better in a dark interior.

Chapter 2
BLOCK AND STONE FOUNDATIONS
MADE EASY

Nothing sets off a dollhouse better than a brick or stone base. Brick and stonework give a feeling of durable strength, and they create a tangible solid foundation which firmly establishes the house in space. If you have a dollhouse that does not have a foundation, adding one is not difficult and the results are very pleasing. It can be created simply by making a frame out of 1" x 2" furring strips. After it has been finished with block or stone in the manner described in this chapter, the foundation can be attached to the dollhouse with Elmer's Wood Glue (see Figure 2-2). If the dollhouse already has the usual two or three inch base, the simple addition of stone corner blocks, or quoins, can also be very attractive.

What I recommend for stonework is *Robinson's Styrofoam Technique*. It has worked well for me over many years and never ceases to win praises for its realistic effect. The maximum expense for this "stonework", on most houses, is only about $3 for structural materials and a little more for joint compound. Furthermore, very little weight will be added to the dollhouse.

Figure 2-1 The real fieldstone foundation of this house adds a touch of authenticity to the overall look. Part II explains how to create a similar foundation for your house.

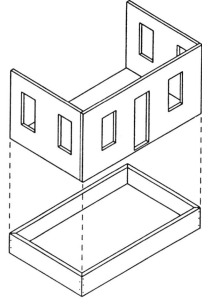

Figure 2-2 The frame measures the same as the house size, however do not attach it until the block or stonework is done.

Materials and Tools

Though this stone foundation uses a construction method similar to my bricklaying technique, you will not need the same basic materials or tools. Here are the major changes: you will need to use a contact bond glue rather than a wood glue; foundation blocks are made from styrofoam rather than from wooden stirrers; and you will need a few C-clamps. Most items can be purchased at any hobby and/or hardware store, however not every item listed will be needed for each project. Read my instructions before making any purchases.

C-clamps (size needed will depend on the height of the foundation wall)
Contact bond glue—use for gluing two unlike surfaces together
Pencil
Ruler
Razor blade or sharp knife
Scrap wood (small flat piece)
Joint compound (either a dry or premixed compound)
Styrofoam coffee cups

PART I — CONCRETE FOUNDATIONS AND CORNER BLOCKS

While very stark looking, by far, the greater percentage of houses have a simple concrete block foundation. In Figure 2-3 are the two most common arrangements of concrete blocks, and it is these that I explain how to do. Other arrangements are seen less frequently, but the techniques described in this section can be applied to them. However, it may be wise to at least experiment with the simpler foundations before attempting the more difficult.

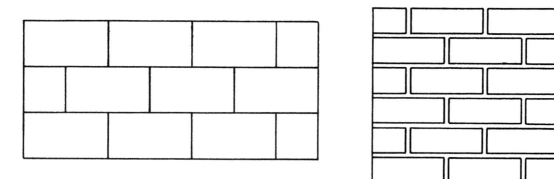

Figure 2-3 Simple concrete block arrangements.

Cutting the Stones

Gather together a quantity of styrofoam coffee cups, the kind used in carry-out food stores. Then with an X-acto knife cut the styrofoam into small rectangles of approximately one-half by three-quarters of an inch. After a few have been cut, place them across the base of the house. Stand back and look at their effect. Are they in perspective with the house? Should they be smaller or bigger? Should they butt up one against the other, or would they look better with some space between them? It is no less important that the foundation fit the style of the house than it is that the roof does.

When planning the foundation be aware that the stones on each row will alternate in the same way that bricks do on a wall. However, unlike the process of laying bricks in the chimney section, instead of cutting off overhanging bricks, here you will make a special stone which will wrap around the corner. This is explained below.

Once comfortable with the size of the stones, go back and mass-produce as many as needed. It is always a good idea to test-fit them along the dollhouse base in a uniform pattern of two or three rows before you glue them down. However, here is a hint—you may find it easier to plan your layout on a life-size drawing of the base since the actual frame can be clumsy with which to work.

Applying the Stones

The corners are more difficult to apply than the rows. They are, therefore, a good place to start. The corner blocks should be cut one half longer than the other blocks because they will wrap around the corner of the frame.

To make the corner bend, place the piece of styrofoam on a flat surface and, on the backside, measure off two-thirds. Then lightly score a crease across the width with your fingernail dividing the styrofoam into two-thirds on one side of the crease and one-third on the other (see Figure 2-4). Do not be upset if a few rectangles crack in the process. Styrofoam is strong and excellent for holding liquids, but it is also brittle and will break with too much pressure. However with a little practice you can master the art of stone-making.

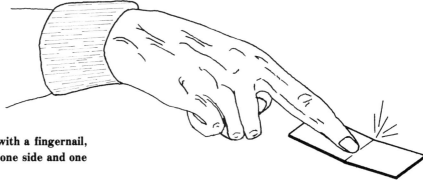

Figure 2-4 Score the styrofoam blocks with a fingernail, dividing it into two parts—two thirds on one side and one third on the other.

Once the stones have been cut, use a good wood glue to apply them. I like Elmer's Wood Glue; others may prefer Elmer's Glue-All, but in any case, a *non-flammable* type must be used that will not dissolve the styrofoam.

Starting at a lower corner, apply a dab of glue to one side of the dollhouse, then place the styrofoam corner piece on it with the crease coming to the edge (See Figure 2-5A). Lightly clamp it to the building with a C-clamp, but before tightening, place a thin piece of scrap wood between the styrofoam and the clamp to protect the foam (Figure 2-5B). Be sure that you tighten the clamp screw slowly. Too much pressure or uneven pressure will dent or shift the foam. After the first side has dried, bend the styrofoam around the corner (Figure 2-5C) and repeat the gluing-clamping process (Figure 2-5D).

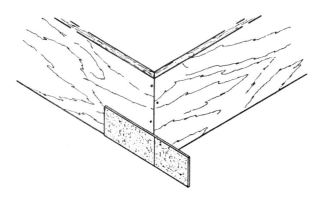

Figure 2-5A Glue the styrofoam on with the scored line coming to the edge. Remember that the long part goes on the front and rear of the foundation.

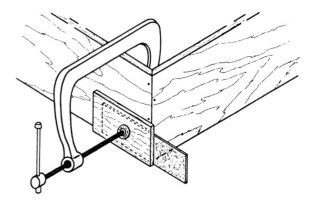

Figure 2-5B Gently clamp a small strip of wood over the styrofoam.

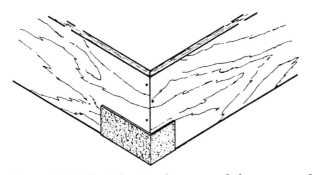

Figure 2-5C Bend the styrofoam around the corner and glue it down.

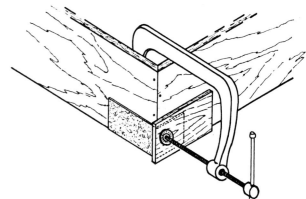

Figure 2-5D Repeat the clamping process.

For the next row up, reverse the styrofoam so that a butt stone is over a long stone. Do all the corners, alternating each row in this manner (see Figure 2-6). Remember, a row that starts with a full stone should end with a full stone, and the same goes for rows that start with butt stones. To even up the blocks if they do not line up straight after they are in place, take a razor blade or sharp knife and trim them with a firm, but light cut.

Fill in the areas between the corners with the regular size blocks. If you planned well, all the styrofoam pieces should fit in perfectly. If a few do not fit, trim them with a razor. The slight difference in block size should not be noticeable.

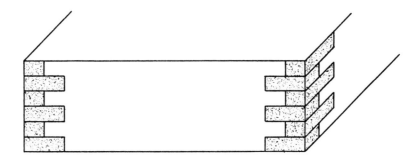

Figure 2-6 Finish the corners by alternating the blocks, short over long.

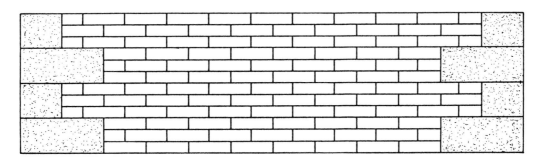

Figure 2-7 Bricks lined up between concrete blocks makes for an attractive wall.

To complete the project, fill in the cracks with joint compound and then wipe off the excess. The white foundation can be painted with a latex paint to match the house color or left as is. Either way will look fine though the effect will be somewhat different.

To add some personality to your dollhouse a handsome type of outside wall can be built by placing the blocks on just the corners of the house and arranging bricks on the walls between. This is a very popular building style, and there are many examples of it to study in most older communities.

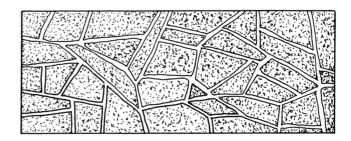

Figure 2-8 Foundations and walls can also be made with odd-shaped styrofoam blocks.

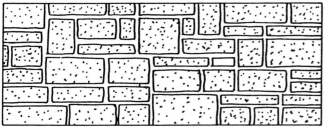

Other interesting foundations can be created with blocks that are not cut exactly square. In fact, a pleasing rustic effect can be achieved by cutting the styrofoam into various shapes and sizes to resemble fieldstones. The blocks can be painted gray (use a non-flammable latex paint only) and the joints filled in afterwards to give the look of real fieldstone. In any case, use the style which best fits your house, and be patient in working through each of the steps.

PART II — USING REAL FIELDSTONE

Real stone on a miniature foundation can add a delightful touch of authenticity to a dollhouse. It will be necessary to spend some additional time on the project, however, as shown in Figure 2-1, the effect is very worthwhile.

The stones for your project can be readily found in a gravel driveway or along a creek in the woods. Keep in mind while looking that each stone must have at least one flat side.

After having gathered a pile of small, flat and relatively thin stones, lay them out on a life-size drawing of the foundation. Figure 2-9 shows examples of some common wall layouts. Note that each stone complements its neighbor's shape and fits together like pieces in a jigsaw puzzle. You want to do the same to eliminate large gaps.

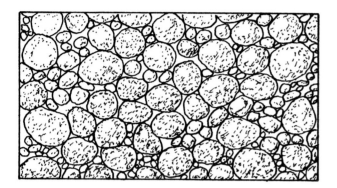
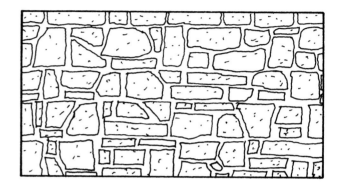

Figure 2-9 Common fieldstone arrangements.

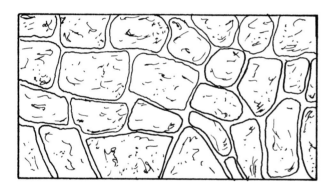

When doing the corners in particular, you will need to pay some extra attention to the fit. It looks best if the stones meet evenly at the edge of the wall, rather than having a few hang over. Work the stones in as tight an interlocking grid as possible. It will give a more finished, professional and substantial look to the stonework.

There are several ways to apply stones. One way is with contact bond glue. In most cases simply coat the dollhouse base with the glue and apply a dab to each stone before transferring it from the drawing to its place on the wall. Make sure to read the manufacturer's instructions for any special application techniques and glue-setting time.

There is also a helpful little secret of the trade which involves a one-step, quick process for applying stones which I will pass on to you. There is a product called *Liquid-Nail* which is obtainable at most hardware stores. Simply follow the instructions on the label and you should not go wrong.

After the stones have been applied, use joint compound to fill in the spaces and simulate mortar. For added realism, mix in a little food coloring (red and green will produce brown) and/or fine sand to age the appearance of the mortar. It would be a good

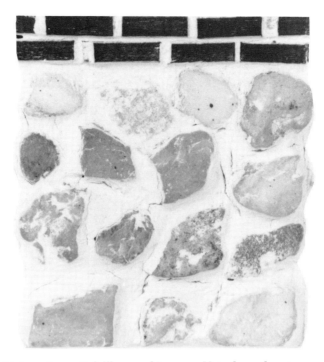

Figure 2-10 The fieldstone base of dollhouse chimney. Note how the stones evenly meet at edge.

idea to experiment with the "weathered" mortar by first testing it on a scrap piece of wood. Let it dry before you evaluate the effect.

Flat, smooth stones are easy to work with, and after applying, excess mortar can be readily wiped clean with a damp cloth. On the other hand, I have always liked the effect of a many-faceted rock (see Figure 2-11), but it is more difficult to wipe excess mortar from this kind of rough surface. In this case, let the mortar dry thoroughly before wiping and then use a stiff wire brush to clean off the excess. Because of the wait during the drying time, the rough stone walls will require a day or so longer to complete.

Keep in mind that if real stones are used, they will be adding weight to the house, and it will be necessary to work with a bonding glue. While it is the best glue to use for two unlike surfaces, once something is attached it is there to stay! I would suggest experimenting with a few stones on a piece of scrap wood before tackling the dollhouse.

Another reminder is that the mortar will probably have to applied twice in many places, due to the shrinkage that normally occurs in the drying process. Look for small cracks where the mortar covers large gaps between the rocks. Take a small dab of mortar on a finger and work it into the cracks to smooth them out.

Fieldstones can also be used very effectively on chimneys. Using the same techniques as described above, an entire chimney could be covered with stones, or, as seen on many older real chimneys, a combination of stone and brick looks good. Search out houses in your area to find some examples of stone chimneys to aid you in your planning.

Chapter 3
FLOORING FEATS

PART I—Plank-type flooring: particularly appropriate for Colonial, Civil War and Early American homes, but can be used in almost any type of house; should be classified as the most common.

PART II—Simulated Oak flooring: suggested for shadow boxes, room boxes and any unbuilt dollhouse; a general purpose floor that will go with any decor.

PART III—Random flooring (prescribed sheet): can be used in any type of dollhouse, built or unbuilt; best suited for Colonial but will go with any decor.

PART IV—Parquet flooring: a high-class floor; the final touch to a Victorian house.

PART V—Thresholds (for doorways and openings)

PART VI—Tips for laying floors in finished dollhouses.

This how-to chapter on flooring projects supplies the dollhouse builder with the knowledge needed to create, in miniature, floors which they would be delighted to have in their own homes. We will look at four types of floors along with step-by-step instructions for installation. Read the text through and study the pictures. Become familiar with the entire project before beginning to work. A flooring job should not be done haphazardly.

Choosing the flooring which best suits your type of house can be critical, especially if it is supposed to represent a particular time period. I would suggest that you examine some pictures of real finished floors. At the beginning of each flooring section I have noted several types of houses that might use that floor.

Figure 3-1   A well-made wooden floor enhances any room scene.

Just how much time and effort is spent on the floor is, of course, for the builder to decide, but it should be pointed out that I have added those extra touches which, when included, will result in a very close replica of the real thing.

Although all of my methods are applicable to the dollhouse-in-progress, I also explain how to overcome the problems of laying a floor in a house which has already been built and finished with trim, doors and wallpaper.

All of the finished floors in the pictures were given a coat of light fruitwood stain to darken the wood and one coat of shellac to bring out the grain and add luster. This was done to better photograph details, but of course the choice of stain and finish is up to the builder. Please note that once shellac is applied to a floor, it cannot be sanded. If you feel that you might do some sanding later, use lacquer.

Tools

Only these few basic tools are needed to complete any of the flooring projects. However, not all of them are needed for each project. Read the instructions before making any purchases:

X-acto fine tooth saw
X-acto miter box
X-acto knife or razor blade
Fine grit sandpaper
Medium grit sandpaper
Elmer's Wood Glue
Contact Bond Glue
Four 3" wood clamps
Waxed paper
3/4" scrap wood approx. 2' long

Materials (NOTE: Each of the four flooring materials mentioned here is used for only one type of floor.)
1/16" thick x 3/8" to 1" wide basswood strips (used for plank flooring)
Wooden coffee stirrers (used for simulated oak flooring)
Random flooring 1/16" x 3-1/2" x 22". Manufactured by Northeastern Scale Models.
Parquet floor 2" x 6" squares. Manufactured by Houseworks, Ltd.

Before proceeding, it would be best to get some important *do's* and *don'ts* out of the way:

Do not force any flooring into place. Leave a slight gap of about 1/32" around the edges where the floor meets the walls. Even though no one will be walking on these floors, expansion and contraction will take place and a section of floor could buckle.

Do not try to make full runs through doorways or archways. Work one room at a time (this applies only to the built dollhouse). The main reason for not making a full run is the limited space in which one has to work, as well as trying to match a floor in the next room. The break between the rooms can be finished with a threshold, just like a real house.

Do not use extra weight to hold the floor down on the built dollhouse. Three of the four floors described use contact bond glue and no extra weight is needed.

Do remember to always start at the open part of the dollhouse or the part first visible and work inward. Any unusual cuts that you may have to make in order to get the wood to fit into the last row will be less obvious.

PART I — PLANK FLOORING

Plank flooring is a very standard type found in a large variety of houses and was very popular in homes that date back to earlier times. Although I would almost definitely use this style for Early American period dollhouses, do not feel limited, many houses today are having pine plank flooring installed in a trend to recreate a feeling of Americana that will probably continue for some time to come.

Figure 3-2 Close-up of a stained basswood plank floor.

Either of two types of basswood, smooth or rough, are used. However the installation method described is the same for both. While a rough floor would look best in an Early American or colonial-type dollhouse, a smooth floor would be fine in a house of almost any period.

Before you get into the actual laying of a dollhouse plank floor, I think it is important for you to understand how the construction methods of real floors dictate how they will look.

When one builds a real house, parallel beams of wood which span the length of the house are set in place before the floor is put down (see Figure 3-3). These beams, called *joists*, are set 16 or 24 inches apart, and the subfloor and finished floor are laid on top, with the planks running perpendicular to the beams. In old houses there usually is no subfloor and the finished planks are nailed directly to the joists.

Hence, in order to make the strongest floor possible, with planks that do not bend, each end of a plank must rest directly over a joist. This means that the length of the planks is

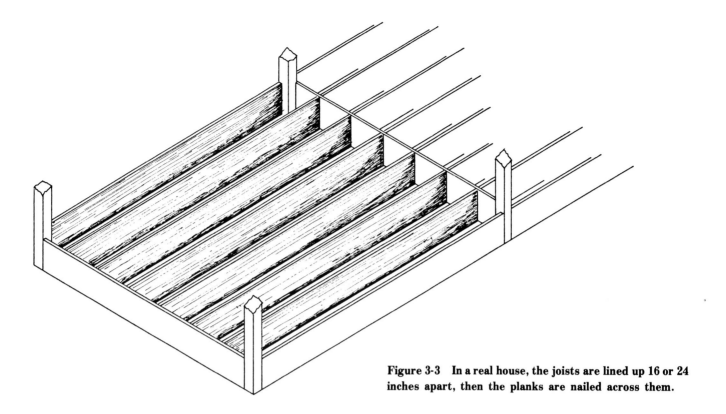

Figure 3-3 In a real house, the joists are lined up 16 or 24 inches apart, then the planks are nailed across them.

dictated by the distance between joists. (For example, if the joists are placed 24 inches apart, you would use planks whose lengths are cut in multiples of 24 inches—they would be 24 inches long, or 48 inches, or 72 inches, etc.) Because the planks must conform to that certain length, very attractive symetrical patterns can be created by staggering the breaks between planks.

Now, it is not necessary to set in joists for your dollhouse, but it is necessary that you be aware of their theoretical existence when laying out the floor. So first off, draw a set of parallel lines across the area to be covered. These lines will be your joists. To prevent from using planks which are too short, and which subsequently cause breaks that are too close together, it would be best to scale your dollhouse floor as if the joists were actually 24 inches apart in a full-sized house. In most dollhouses this would mean that the lines will be drawn at 2 inch intervals (see Figure 3-4).

You may have to shift the joist lines a little so that you do not end up with a very short distance between the last joist and the wall—a good range would be about 1" or more left over. Play with the lines until they fit well, even if it means also starting with less than two inches.

Please note that these lines do not have to be used; however, they keep the breaks spaced exactly and do help to add a nice touch of realism.

Start by working a few rows at a time, cutting and setting the sticks of wood in place as you go. Do not glue at this time—making this floor is like constructing a jigsaw puzzle and you want to be sure that you have a perfect fit before you affix anything permanently. Remember to leave a 1/32" space around the edge of the entire area to allow for

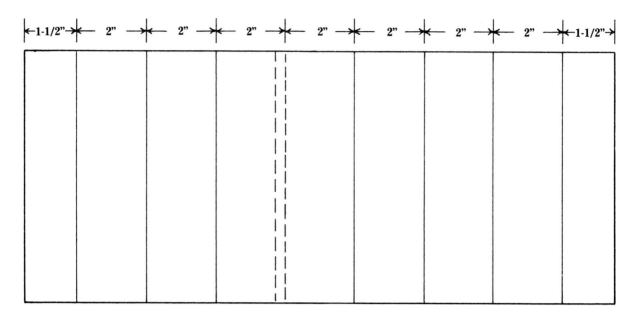

Figure 3-4 Draw joist lines across the dollhouse floor.

expansion and contraction, and stagger the boards so that the breaks between ends occur randomly. A full board here and there mixed into the rows is acceptable, although on a real floor a full board is not very common.

Again, begin from the outside of the dollhouse and work inwards, the last piece or row can be cut to fit, and a very narrow piece will not be as noticeable inside as it would be on the outside edge.

Over time, real boards in older period homes tend to shrink and a small space develops between them. To give that more authentic look to your miniature floor, cut up some

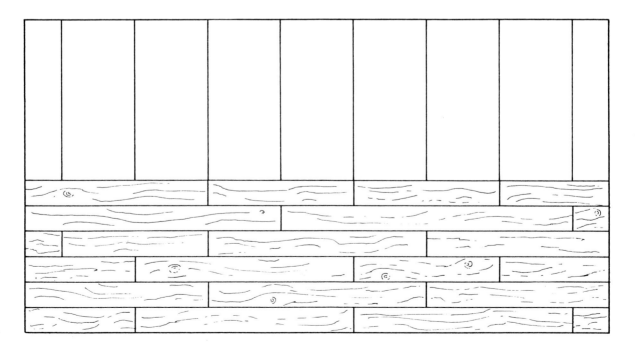

Figure 3-5 Note that the planks begin and end on a joist line.

matchbook covers and insert them between the planks. Do so on the ends and along the sides, then set the planks as close together as they will go. Hold on to the matchbook spacers, you will use them again when you glue down the floor.

The above procedures should be followed whether the dollhouse has its walls in place, or not. If you do not have walls encumbering you, the floor can be laid straight across the entire house. However if that is not the case, lay each room as a separate unit; the threshold between rooms will be dealt with later.

Once the entire floor is laid out, you are ready to stain the planks. It is much easier to stain the planks individually than to try to stain them after the floor has been glued down. This way you can be sure to cover the edges as well as the top surface, and you do not have the danger of splattering on the walls.

As you remove the planks from the dollhouse floor for staining, be sure to lay them out again in the same order as they dry.

As far as a color choice goes, the wooden stirrers will take any kind of stain, light or dark. The floor of a Colonial house looks very good with a fruitwood stain, while a much darker shade, such as walnut, suits a Victorian home. Experiment on some scrap wood with various shades before you stain all the planks. Apply several coats on some, and, on others, let the stain soak in for different periods of time before wiping off. Each of these techniques will achieve a different look.

With all of the above preparation done, you are ready to glue down the floor.

The best adhesive I have found to glue down plank flooring is Elmer's Wood Glue. Be sure to follow the manufacturer's instructions.

Work only a few rows at a time, placing glue on both the wood strip and the floor. Be patient and careful—an advantage to using contact glue is that a large area can be put down quickly and no clamps or weights are needed, but once a piece is down, it is there to stay. Remember, a mistake can be costly.

Also, do not forget to use the matchbook covers again if you have decided to create a space between planks.

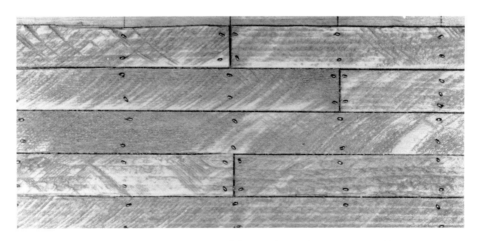

Figure 3-6 **This floor was constructed from pine strips cut on a table top saw from a scrap piece of 3/4" pine. Note the railroad spikes nailed into the planks.**

33

It is not unusual for things to turn out slightly different when the planks are glued down, as opposed to when they are simply laid out. Therefore, you may have to re-cut the last row of wood strips to fit.

If your house already has its walls in place, it would be best at this point to leave the room openings and archways alone until all the molding and trim is in place and doors hung. Once that is done, a simple threshold piece can be made from a strip of flooring cut to fit between the door posts. See Part V for details on constructing thresholds.

A nice touch of realism which can be easily added and looks particularly good on rough cut finished floors is to have nails at the appropriate places above the joists (see Figure 3-6). HO scale model railroad spikes make very authentic looking miniature nails and can be found in most hobby stores which carry model railroading items.

Finally, the floor can be waxed with paste wax or a coat of shellac can be applied.

PART II — SIMULATED OAK FLOORING

A simulated oak floor can be installed only on the flat surface of an uncompleted dollhouse before any of the walls go up. While it is a very time-consuming project, keep in mind that the cost is only about three dollars and the results are simply beautiful. Room boxes, in which space is limited, particularly benefit from this type of floor.

Figure 3-7 Close-up of a stained simulated oak floor.

The method described below is of my own invention, and I suggest that you read all the instructions and follow them carefully. Do not attempt to cut corners. I have laid this floor in a number of dollhouses and room boxes and have found all the steps to be essential.

The tools needed for this project are: four C-clamps (or wood clamps), an X-acto fine tooth saw, a flat scrap piece of 3/4" board as long as a row of wood strips and six or seven rows wide, Elmer's Wood Glue and waxed paper.

A simulated oak floor is not really made of oak, but of pine coffee stirrers. They are the same kind of coffee stirrers used in making bricks and, as mentioned, can be found in convenience stores that sell coffee by the cup. Usually you can negotiate with the manager to procure a box for a dollar or two.

Sort through the coffee stirrers and select the straightest ones. Hold aside the ones with knots and blemishes to be later worked into the rows. A real floor has these defects and it will add to the realism.

Unlike with the plank floors (in Part I), it is not necessary to mark off exact joist lines before laying down this oak style floor. Real oak or hardwood floors are laid on top of a subfloor, and the hardwood surface strips are nailed sideways and fitted together with a tongue and groove.

Check out a real hardwood floor and you will notice that the breaks between boards are staggered from row-to-row. When you lay out your floor, do the same. But, remember, you need not create the symmetrical pattern that other plank floors require as real oak planks are not nailed to joists. It is still a good idea to draw several lines along the dollhouse base (see Figure 3-8) to guide your rows, as wooden stirrers tend not to be uniformly straight.

Figure 3-8 Draw guidelines across the dollhouse floor.

The planks for this floor can be any variety of lengths. Trim off the rounded ends on the coffee stirrers, and then cut the stirrers down to random lengths. Even the full length of the coffee stirrer will be fine here and there.

Since there are no walls to contend with, there is no need to be concerned with laying out the floor before it is glued in place. Planks which turn out to be too long and hang over at the edges should be layed as is. The excess will be trimmed off after the glue has dried.

The permanent installation of these "hardwood" planks is a very simple process and requires more patience than anything else as you wait for the glue to dry.

To start, squeeze a thread of glue along one side of a stick and lay it into place, starting with the row closest to the open side of your dollhouse. Start from the middle and work across to the right and left. Continue with the next row, starting at a different point so that the breaks in the boards do not line up. Do the same for five or six rows (see Figure 3-9).

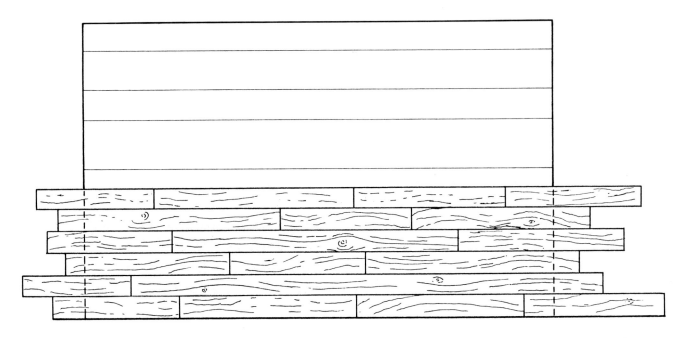

Figure 3-9   Lay five or six rows of planks down. The overhanging pieces will be trimmed after the glue has dried.

Do not cut any overhanging planks at this point. It is not unusual for the sticks to curl up. They will flatten out when the board is clamped on, as explained below.

After all the sticks are glued within an area, lay waxed paper over the sticks (this will prevent the scrap board from becoming stuck to the floor). Place the scrap board on top, and clamp it down at each end and at several points along the middle if dealing with a long floor (see Figure 3-10). Be careful not to disturb the sticks.

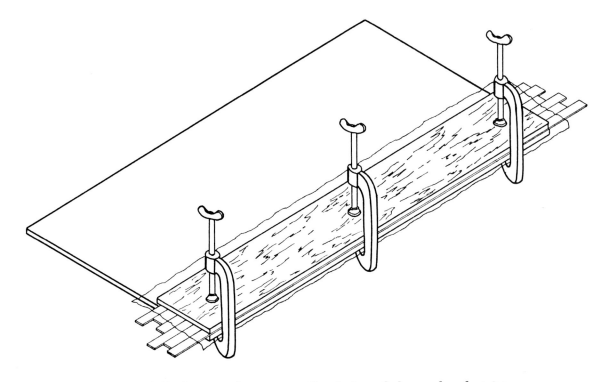

Figure 3-10   Lay waxed paper over the planks and clamp a board on top.

After approximately ten minutes, remove the clamps, board and waxed paper. The glue should have set enough to hold the planks down, yet still be tacky where it may have come through the cracks. Wipe the excess glue off with a damp cloth.

Repeat the process with another five or six rows and continue until the entire board is completed.

If you are laying a wide floor in which the clamps will not reach the middle, crisscross an additional board, such as a thin piece of 1/4" plywood, over top the first, then clamp the sides (See Figure 3-11). This will help to put pressure on the unclamped portion.

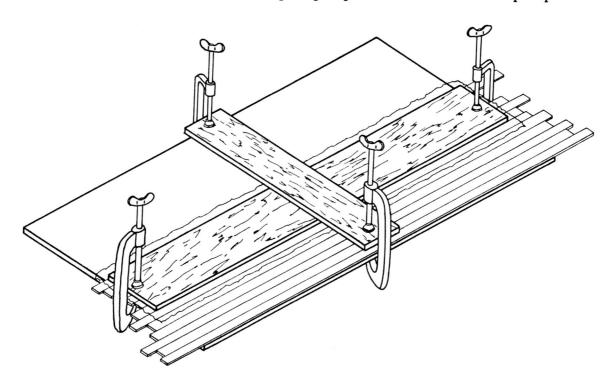

Figure 3-11 On a wide floor, you may have to crisscross another board over top of the first in order to firmly hold down the center planks.

Do not be concerned with cracks between the rows. Some boards will bump together tightly, while between others there will be a gap.

Cut off the overhanging pieces as each section dries and work them into the rows. In a real floor short pieces are used. Also, do not forget to use some of the sticks with knots in them, they add to the character of the floor.

When the floor is finished and the glue well dried, sand the entire area with medium grit sandpaper. Do not blow off the dust! Wipe it off, letting the excess dust settle into the cracks.

The floor is now ready for an application of stain, however, let me make a strong suggestion! Use a light or possibly a medium stain, but do not use a dark stain because that will be defeating the purpose. Remember that the goal is to simulate oak flooring while using pine sticks, hence a light stain will achieve the simulated oak look. Use scrap sticks to try out several stains.

Several things can be done as a final step. A coat of shellac gives a nice shine, and paste wax can be added to that also.

See Part V in this chapter to learn how doorways and openings can be finished using a tongue depressor.

PART III — RANDOM FLOORING (Prescribed Sheet)

A Random Floor is one of the quickest to install. The one I have used for this text is manufactured by Northeastern Scale Models and comes in 1/16" x 3-1/2" x 22" sheets with scribed lines to simulate floor boards.

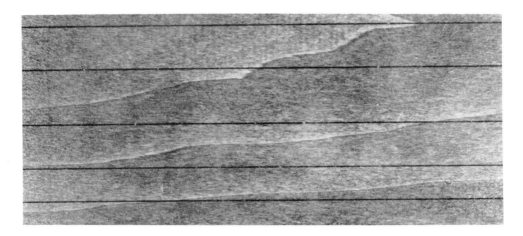

Figure 3-12 Close-up of stained random flooring.

Since the board comes in 3-1/2" wide sheets, the first thing that you will have to do is cut several strips to fit the length and shape of the room. Remember to allow for a 1/32" gap on all edges which meet a wall. Lay them out on the floor as you go to check the fit.

Stain the flooring as desired, making certain that the scribed lines are well covered with stain—they will darken and stand out better. It is important to flood the lines so that the light wood does not bleed through on places that have been missed. Wipe off any excess.

Do not panic if a sheet bows after it is stained. It will flatten out again when it is glued in place.

Use a contact bond glue. With a brush, coat both the base of the dollhouse and the underside of the flooring. Be careful and make sure that the flooring has been cut just right—with this type of glue you get only one chance. Once the flooring is in place, it is in place to stay. Coat the floor an extra inch or so around the area where the piece is to go. This will allow you to lay the next piece of flooring without having to brush glue on the base so close to the first piece, thus keeping it clean.

A tip on laying this type of floor: grasp the piece of flooring between both hands, thumbs on the bottom, index fingers on top pushing the center so that you bend the wood slightly. This way the flooring can be shifted as needed and rolled into place. *CAUTION!* Do not curve the floor too much, just enough to get the bend.

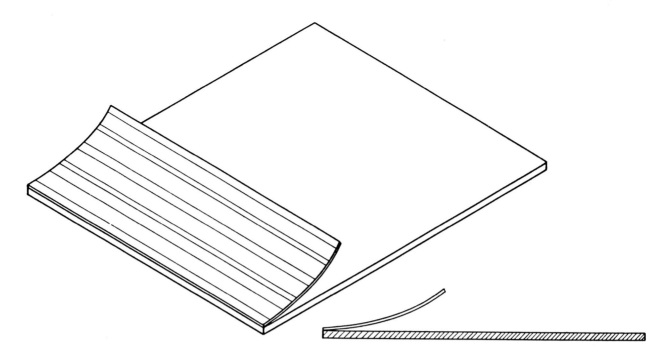

Figure 3-13A Line the board up against the floor edge and roll it into place.

For the first piece, place your thumbs against the dollhouse base edge and, holding the flooring on an angle, even up the flooring edge with the base edge. When both edges feel even, roll the flooring down. Continue on, bumping up one board tightly with the next, and then rolling the piece out as described above.

Random flooring can be left with just the stain or it can be covered with shellac and wax.

To finish any room openings such as doorways and archways, turn to Part V.

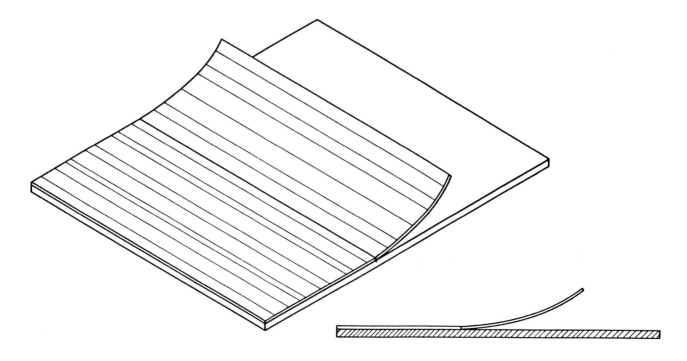

Figure 3-13B Bump the second board tightly against the first and roll it into place.

PART IV — PARQUET FLOORING

A Parquet Floor is one of the finest you can put into a dollhouse and one of the most expensive. However, if you are looking for a first class floor, this is it.

Figure 3-14 Close-up of stained parquet flooring.

I suggest that you start out by experimenting with Parquet flooring by laying it in a small area, such as a room box. This will give you a chance to become adept at working with Parquet flooring at a minimum expense, while at the same time let you create a really special scene.

The type of flooring which I use is made by Houseworks Ltd. of Atlanta, Georgia. They have four different patterns to choose from and the one shown in Figure 14 is the

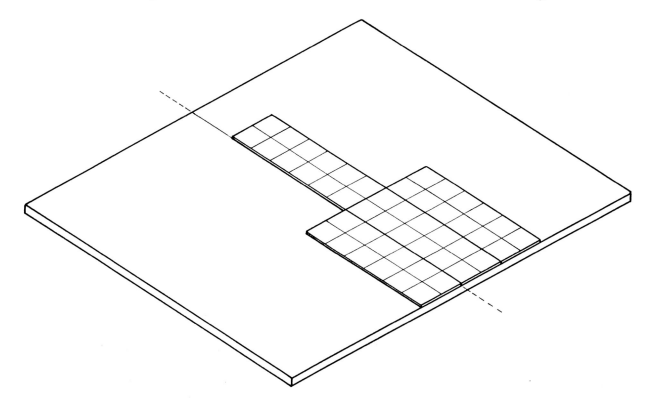

Figure 3-15 Cover the floor working outward from a center line.

basket-weave pattern. The flooring comes packaged in 2" x 6" sheets, and will cover twelve square inches.

The only tool you will need is an X-acto knife or razor blade.

To start, measure the area to be covered to determine the amount of flooring needed. Divide the room in half and draw a line down the center to guide you as you lay the floor.

Beginning at the center, without gluing, lay out the sections of flooring working in both directions (see Figure 3-15). Now, it would be nice if the room was just the right size so that the sections come out evenly all the way around, but chances are they will not. In most cases the edges will have to be cut to fit.

Figure 3-16   Trimming parquet flooring.

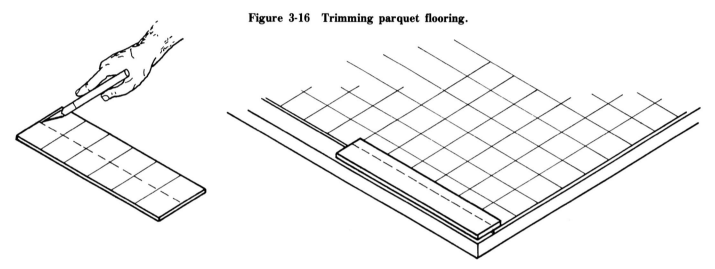

A. Split a strip of flooring in half if necessary.

B. Lay the strip in place and draw a line where it overlaps the other flooring.

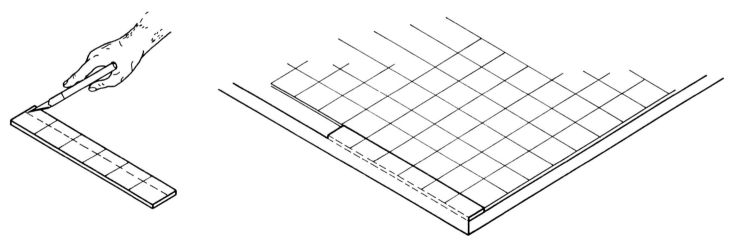

C. Cut the strip along the line.

D. Turn the cut strip around and lay in place.

It would be ideal if those edges of the floor needing to be covered were to come out to an inch or less. Since the flooring comes in 2" sections and cuts in half fairly easy at the joints, it would be most economical since one piece could be used for completing two rows. If this is the case, *do* cut the section in half before doing further trimming (Figure 3-16A).

Next, lay the piece to be trimmed in place, overlapping the rest of the floor covering (Figure 3-16B). The amount that overlaps will be the amount that you will want to trim. Make marks at the edges of the piece where they meet the body of the floor and draw a line to connect them.

Using the X-acto knife or razor blade and a straight edge, make light cuts along the line until the flooring separates (Figure 3-16C). Do not be alarmed if a section piece falls off, as sometimes happens. Keep the loose piece and glue it into place when the floor is laid.

When you set the cut strip into place and check the trim, turn it around so that the cut-side faces the wall and the smooth uncut side completes the pattern of the rest of the floor (Figure 3-16D). You may need to experiment a bit when starting out, but soon you will get the hang of it.

Remove the floor keeping it in sequence on the work table.

Again starting at the middle, brush a coat of contact bond glue on both the parquet flooring and the dollhouse floor. As with the Random flooring, brush the glue an extra inch or so around the area where the piece is to go to keep all the strips neat and clean.

Press the flooring into its prearranged position, and continue on, working towards the edges.

Remember to keep an eye on the pattern and make sure that all the pieces line up with their neighbor properly. Check the edge pieces before gluing them into place. Sometimes they need to be recut.

Once the glue has dried, sand the floor lightly and wipe the surface. Let the dust settle to fill in the cracks and spaces.

Stain to suit and shellac if desired. A Parquet floor also takes paste wax well, which will enhance the grain more.

To finish the doorways and openings, turn to Part V.

PART V — THRESHOLDS

The threshold is the final piece of flooring to go down and will finish the job. Thresholds balance out a floor in a way that is pleasant to the eye and provide that little bit of a break between rooms that is needed in such small scale projects. By this point, all trim such as door jambs or casings, baseboards or shoe moldings should already have been installed (for more on baseboards and door trim, see Chapter 4—TRIMMING OUT).

There are several things to consider when deciding what type of threshold to construct. Will the entrance to the room be just an opening or will it have a doorway? If you are using a door, will it be a purchased pre-hung door or a self-made one? Check out a threshold in a real house and see how it comes together.

If you have laid a Plank or Random type of flooring, use the same material for the threshold. However, if you have chosen a simulated oak or parquet floor, construct the threshold out of a thin scrap piece of basswood or a tongue depressor.

For entrances between rooms which do not have a door, cut the wood for the threshold to fit just between the opening. The width of the wood will be determined by the width of the wall and the type of trim used. Taper the sides, as shown in Figure 3-18, so that when laid, the edges meet smoothly with the floor.

After the wood is cut, stain it the same shade as the floor, and then glue it into place.

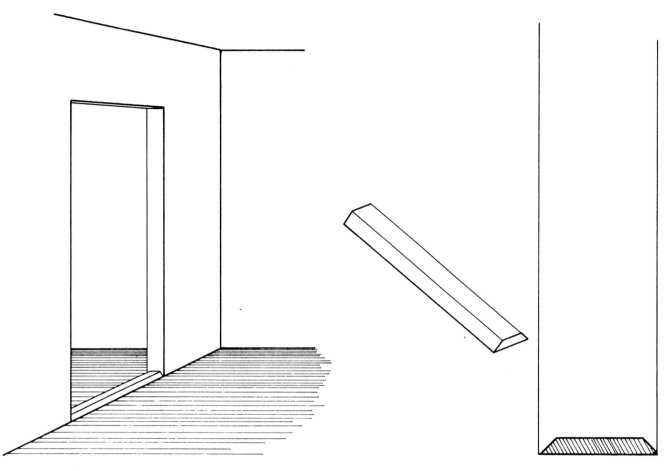

Figure 3-17 A doorway with a threshold dividing the floors of the two rooms.

Figure 3-18 A threshold for an entrance with no door.

A pre-hung door, such as a Houseworks brand, may (and usually does) come in a rectangular frame with a bottom doorstop that will need to be blended in with the floor. To do this, two thin strips of wood will be needed. Trim the strips to meet flush with the height of the doorstop, and cut angles in them so that the sides taper down to the floor (see Figure 3-19).

Figure 3-19 Constructing a threshold for a pre-hung door frame.

43

Before gluing the threshold into place, stain all the pieces, including the doorstop of the pre-hung door frame, to match the floor. Though the woods may not match, when stained they will blend together enough to disappear.

PART VI — TIPS FOR LAYING FLOORS IN A FINISHED HOUSE

While the floor laying instructions given above apply to any dollhouse, laying a new floor in a house which already has the baseboards, trimmings, doors and wallpaper presents some special difficulties. Working around finished areas is slightly troublesome, but it can be done.

First it is necessary to create adequate clearance beneath the doors. Having chosen a flooring, lay a piece of it down and check to see if the door will easily swing over top of it. If it does not, hold the door tightly against the flooring and use an X-acto knife to carefully trim the bottom edge of the door just enough to allow proper clearance. Do not try to cut it all at once—make several cuts to do the job smoothly.

Figure 3-20 Trim the door just above where the new flooring hits it.

Another problem encountered may be the baseboards. If they are only a flat strip of wood around the walls the solution will be simple. The floor can be cut to fit up to the baseboard and 1/4" round toe or shoe molding can be installed to cover the gap between the floor and the wall.

But, if the baseboard already has shoe molding attached, there are two ways in which you can deal with it.

When using a thick floor such as one made of basswood, cut the edges on a 45 degree angle and lay it in place. Then add a new molding strip around the wall to cover the crack (see Figure 3-21).

Figure 3-21 Laying a new floor over old molding.

For a thin floor such as the parquet, the old shoe molding must be removed . Do this very carefully. Lay the new floor on top of the old using the method explained in the Parquet Floor section, and install new strips of 1/4" round.

An important thing to remember is that should the existing floor be painted already, go over it with rough sandpaper before laying any kind of new floor on top. This will be necessary in order to give a good bond with the glue.

Chapter 4
TRIMMING OUT

By the time builders of real houses prepare for the "trimming out," they have finished all major construction (framing, roofing, flooring) and are beginning the time-consuming work which changes a house into a home. The many loose ends are pulled together, windows are installed and door trim applied.

As a dollhouse builder and finisher, I will cover some of the same areas of trimming as in a real house, but I will proceed in a somewhat different order and give greater or lesser priority to certain tasks.

When finishing a real house, painting or papering walls is left to the very end. With dollhouses, however, ceilings and walls should be painted and papered first as separate components, then these surfaces are erected to form a house. It is then easy to glue the trim to finished walls and dollhouse surfaces.

I have divided dollhouse trimmings into five parts: **Part I**—*DOOR TRIM*, **Part II**—*BASEBOARD TRIM*, **Part III**—*WINDOW TRIM*, **Part IV**—*CHAIRRAIL TRIM*, and **Part V**—*CEILING TRIM*.

In each of the sections, all of the trim is made from flat stock which will require only simple cuts. The projects have been designed for the novice, but at the same time, the advice and materials used are suitable for the sophisticated builder of Early American or Colonial dollhouses where straight cuts and flat stock look very appropriate.

Since the separate aspects of your dollhouse are brought together at this point, plan ahead to achieve a consistent overall effect. Now is the time to decide on stain or paint color, trim color, and accessory colors and styles. Even consider the roof color.

A suggestion: I recommend a fruitwood-colored stain for basswood trim. It is not too dark, nor too light. Besides the trimming, it looks nice on other basswood projects, such as basswood flooring (see Chapter 3).

It is important that *all* wooden strips or pieces be stained or painted at one time. This is to insure that all pieces are as close to the same color as possible—almost anytime you deal with colors, one dye lot is apt to be slightly different from another even though they are marked the same. Therefore, it is better to prepare too much stain or paint the first time around rather than too little. From personal experience I have learned this lesson well, that later on it is always difficult to match up that small unpainted surface with the larger painted one.

So, read through this entire chapter and decide what trimming you would like your dollhouse to have and, if you would like them to match, paint or stain the long uncut strips of wood first. Be sure to save any leftover coloring matter, as later you will probably have to do some small touching up where you have cut the wood.

Figure 4-1 Notice how baseboard trimming and a chair rail nicely finish off this room.

Materials and Tools

The tools and materials needed are listed below, however it may not be necessary to buy them all. If you are using a dollhouse kit, some of the materials may have been included. You may find that some materials have been left over from other finishing projects. And, you may feel that you can use my techniques with materials not even mentioned.

X-acto Razor Tooth Saw
X-acto Miter Box
Elmer's Wood Glue

Masking Tape
Several Spring-type Clothespins
Sharp Knife or Razor Blade
Sheet of Fine Grit Sandpaper
Drywall Joint Compound
1/16" x 3/8" Basswood Strips
1/16 x 1/4" Basswood Strips
1/16" x 1/16" Basswood Strips
1/16" x 1/2" Basswood Strips

PART I — DOOR TRIM

When adding trim to your dollhouse, start with the doorways. This way when you do the baseboards, you can make sure that they butt right up against the doorway's side trim strips.

As far as door trimming styles go, in my exploration of real homes I have come across three basic types—the primitive square butt, the traditional 45 degree angle cut, and the Victorian hang-over style (see Figure 4-2). Pick the one that best suits your house.

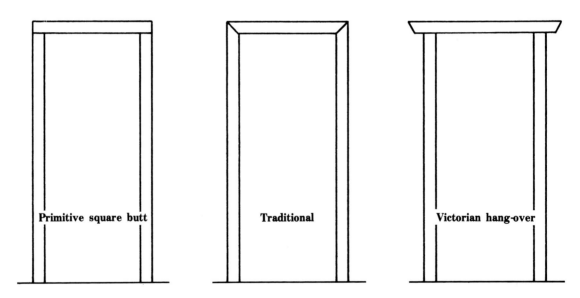

Figure 4-2 Three common styles of door trimming.

Basswood strips of either 1/8", 1/4" or 3/8" width are your best choices for door trimming. To decide which to use, look at the thickness of the walls. If your dollhouse has very thin walls, you would not want to use 3/8" wide strips as they would overwhelm the opening. At the same time, if your dollhouse has thick walls, thin 1/8" strips would become insiqnificant and lost. Hold the different thicknesses against the opening and judge which seems most proper for your dollhouse.

Measure the doorway opening and cut the strips to fit. If you have chosen the Traditional style, an X-acto miter box will make it easy to cut accurate 45 degree angles which will meet tightly. Check the fit and lightly mark their position with a pencil.

You are now ready to glue on the trimming. Start with the top piece over the doorway. Dab glue along the wood strip and press the piece into place. Use masking tape or clothespins to hold it firmly down (see Figure 4-3). This is important as basswood is very thin and tends to warp when moist glue is applied to one side only. Finger pressure will help the glue to set more quickly.

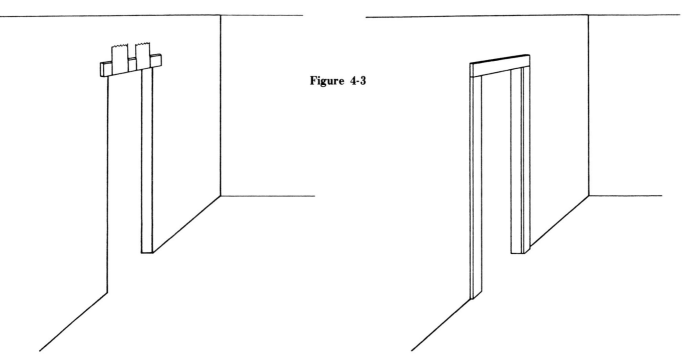

Figure 4-3

A. Use tape to hold the top wood strip in position.   **B. Complete the doorway with the two side strips.**

Handle the side strips in the same way. Once the glue has dried, touch-up the joints with your paint or stain.

With the edges of the opening done, the doorway will look pleasing and present a smooth finish. Later, the door itself can be added.

Just a couple notes of caution: always read the manufacturer's instructions for using glue, particularly if a different type is used than the one I have suggested. If using masking tape, remove it as soon as possible once the trim has adhered to the opening. If left on, the tape could, over time, damage the trim's finish.

PART II — BASEBOARDS

Once the door openings are done, it will become apparent that they needed to be completed before starting other trimming projects. Baseboards, for example, require a finished edge to butt up against.

1/2" x 1/16" basswood strips are usually the best size to use as baseboards. In most dollhouses the 1/2" measurement translates to 6" life-size. This makes the strip particularly well proportioned to the size of most older-style dollhouses.

Beginning with the inside back wall (see Figure 4-4) measure straight across the width of the room and cut a single strip of basswood to fit. If the wall is broken up by a door as

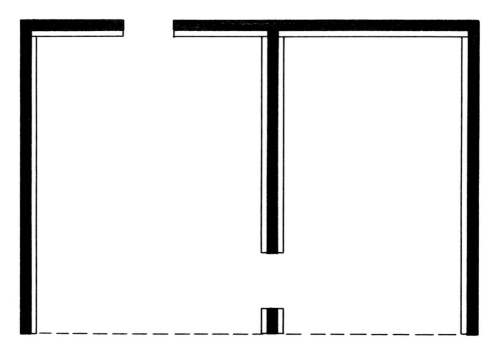

Figure 4-4 Measure for the boards going across the back wall first. At the entrances, the boards should butt right up against the doorway trim.

is the middle wall in the figure, of course, you will need to cut two pieces. Should the strip prove to be a little too long to lay flat, sand away enough of one or both edges so that it fits easily but snugly into place. It is best to cut a strip too long and have to sand it, rather than too short and have gaps at the ends show.

Apply a few dabs of glue to the back side of the baseboard strip and press it firmly into place. Hold it there for several minutes. If, for some reason, the glue does not adhere, use a book as a weight to hold it while the glue sets. Sometimes a long strip springs out at one end and the book will clamp it in place.

Finish the side walls in the same manner. Note that in Figure 4-4 the baseboards are not beveled at 45 degree angles at the corners, but rather the side boards butt flatly against the back board.

Touch up any splintering that has occurred during the cutting with stain or paint.

PART III — WINDOW TRIM

An interesting thing about windows is that it is often not the window itself, but the trimming around it which gives it its character. Even windows with curtains benefit from this small addition when the curtains are pulled back and the little bit of trimming is seen.

While installing window trimming is a relatively simple task, you may run into some problems if working on a custom-built dollhouse or one put together from a kit. They usually come with their own windows and trim, and may not be readily adaptable to your desired trim design. Do not let this stop you—after all, it is your house—but be prepared to put some extra time into the project. You will probably find that 1/16" x 1/2" basswood strips are the best to work with in these cases.

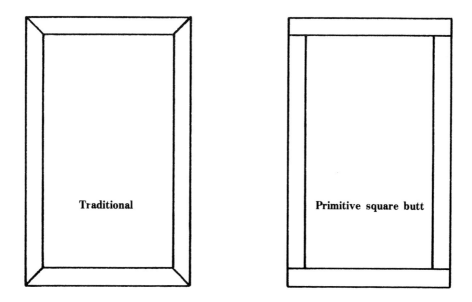

Traditional   Primitive square butt

Figure 4-5 These two common types of window trim match the simple doorway trim shown earlier.

Figure 4-5 shows two simple types of window trim to match the door trim described above. They can be mounted either on top of the window, flush with the wall; or around the window, raised off the wall.

Flush-mounted trim is used for windows that have been set deep into the wall, thereby leaving an outline of unfinished inner-wall going around it. Installation is simple. First, choose the appropriate size basswood (quite likely the same size as was used for the door trim) and cut four pieces so that when put together they will fit snugly within the

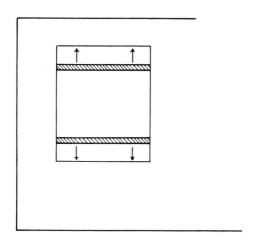

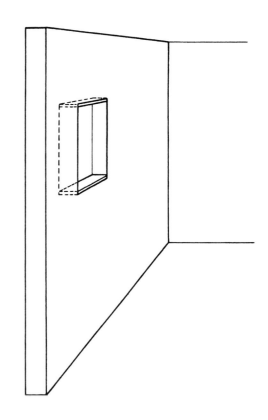

Figure 4-6A   Glue the top and bottom pieces in place.

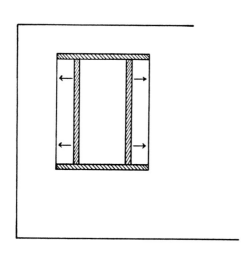

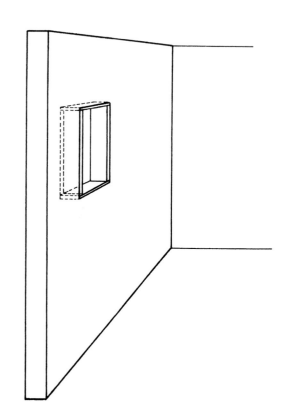

Figure 4-6B   Glue in the side pieces.

circumference of the window area over the glass.   Figure 4-6(A,B,C) diagrams the process. Glue the pieces on in the usual manner. Once in place, you may have to shave the basswood slightly with a razor to make it sit flush with the inner wall. Flush-mounted window trim often looks best if not stained, but painted the same color as the walls.

You may prefer raised window trimming that sits out from the wall a little. In that case you can use the Victorian Hang-Over trim as well as the styles shown in Figure 4-5. The only addition which you will make is a strip to go across the bottom of the window.

As opposed to the way that the basswood is cut for flush-mounted trim, the strips for raised trimming should be cut to fit around the *outside* of the window area. See Figure 4-7 for the process. When glued on, the pieces should meet even with the edge of the window opening. This kind of trimming looks fine stained the same color as the door trimming.

Figure 4-6C   Shave the basswood so that it sits flush with the wall.

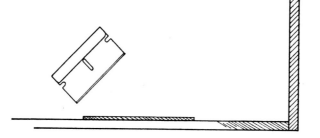

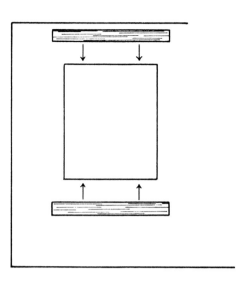

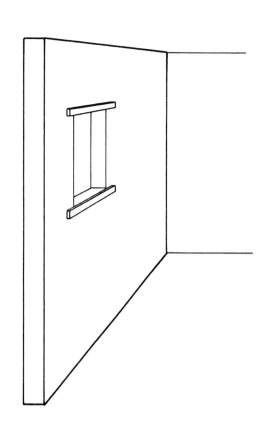

Figure 4-7A   Glue the top and bottom pieces in place.

I want to discuss one more touch which beautifully finishes off a deeply mounted window when using raised trim. Essentially, it is a combination of a flush and raised window trim. Because of that, it takes some extra work, but the results are well worth it.

Before you cut the outer trimming, cut four strips of basswood to fit flatly around the inner window casing (see Figure 4-6). They should be wide enough to meet evenly with the wall. Glue them in; then, cut the outside raised trimming to fit flush with the inner

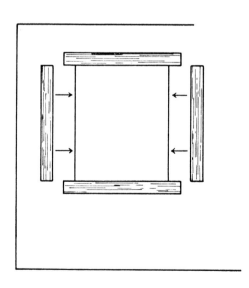

Figure 4-7B   Glue on the side pieces.

pieces (see Figure 4-7). Since all the trimming pieces should have been cut from pre-stained or painted strips, you will need to touch up only a few bare spots.

Figure 4-8 Cutaway of a combination flush and raised window trim.

PART IV — CHAIR RAILS

A wainscot is a lining or paneling, usually made from wood, ceramic tiles or linoleum, which covers just the lower portion of a wall. Running along the top of the wainscot, around the wall, sits a narrow band of wood called a *chair rail*, or wainscot cap. Its function is to prevent chairs from being pushed up against the wall and marring the wainscot, or upper paint or wallpaper. Though usually found in the dining room or kitchen, chair rails can also be a very attractive addition to a den, living room or bedroom.

In this section I will discuss chair rails only. The wainscoting itself will be covered in detail in a future volume, but let me throw out this one suggestion: you can very easily immitate the style of Colonial or Early American interiors in which the walls were typically made of plaster, by finishing the wall below the chair rail with either a neutral colored paint or drywall compound. It might also be a striking decorative accent in a very modern home. It would not, however, be in keeping with a fancy Victorian dining room.

Staying with the plain flat trim that we have been putting on, plan on using the 1/16" x 3/8" basswood strips. They should be stained or painted before they are applied.

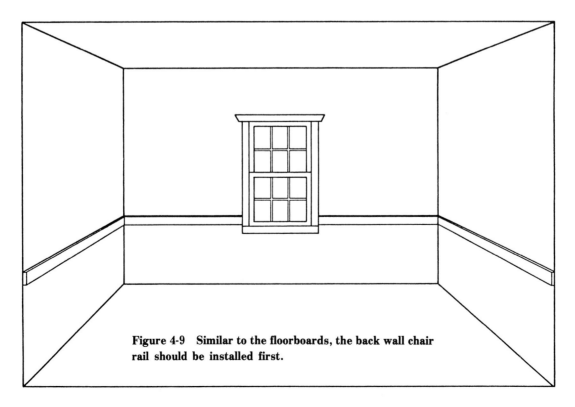

Figure 4-9 Similar to the floorboards, the back wall chair rail should be installed first.

Begin with the back wall or with the one farthest away from the dollhouse's open side. Using a ruler, draw a light line from end to end at about 2-1/2" above the floor. Place several of your miniature chairs along the line to make sure that it matches with the height of the chair backs—remember the purpose of chair rails. Adjust the height to suit, then continue the line across the side walls.

Next, cut a length of basswood strip for the back wall so that it fits snugly. Sand off any rough edges. Dab the strip with glue and place it in position. Hold it there for a few minutes until the glue begins to set. If windows or built-in cabinets break the wall, use several strips and butt the rails tightly against them.

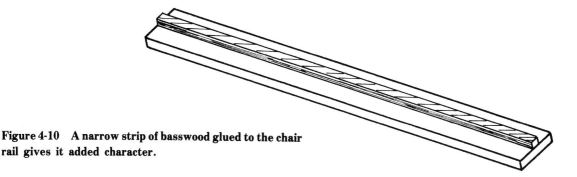

Figure 4-10 A narrow strip of basswood glued to the chair rail gives it added character.

Do the side walls starting from the corners and working out toward the opening. Figure 4-9 shows how the chair rail should look. Finally, touch up any exposed areas with stain.

To accentuate the chair rail's effect, cut another strip of basswood, this time 1/16" x 1/16", and glue it directly along the center of the first strip (see Figure 4-10). Do not forget to stain it to match the rest of the rail first. The second piece will add dimension to the first piece and give it character.

PART V — CEILING TRIM

The ceiling is the last area to be trimmed in the house and will complete the job. Thought to be a relatively unimportant trim, if only because it is the least observed and, therefore, the least appreciated, in a room that is spacious and well lighted, ceiling trim acts to balance it off quite tastefully. And, it subdues the ceiling and walls so that they do not overpower the setting. In addition, ceiling trim serves the purpose of hiding the rough edges where the wallpaper and ceiling meet.

Use 3/8" x 1/16" strips of basswood so that the ceiling trim conforms with the other trim described in this chapter. (There are, however, many types of decorative ceiling trim on the market.) Ceiling trim should be applied along the top of the wall. This way the room retains its height while still gaining a decorative border.

Just as with the baseboards, ceiling trim should be applied first along the back wall, and then along the sides. Measure across the back wall and cut a single strip of basswood to length. Remember when cutting any wood, that it is easier to sand off a couple fractions of an inch to get a tight fit, than it is to add on those fractions to fill in a gap. So always cut the wood a little longer than your measurements call for, and then sand.

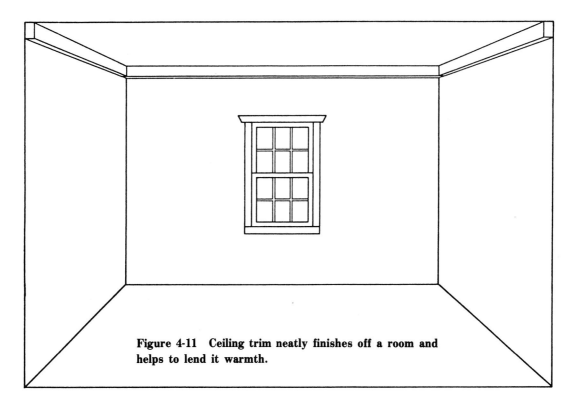

Figure 4-11 Ceiling trim neatly finishes off a room and helps to lend it warmth.

Apply glue to the piece and press it into place on the ceiling; again because of the tendency of the wood to bend, you may have to hold it there until the glue sets. Then measure the side walls from the back ceiling trim to the outside. Cut the wood and apply it as you did the first strip.

The trim should be painted the same color as the ceiling. This should be done before you glue on the strips. I would not recommend staining the trim in wood tones, as the darker lines will give the room a closed-in feeling. *Do not* paint the backside of the strips, glue will not adhere to paint as it does to stain.

After the glue has completely dried, carefully touch up the joints between strips to blend the trim together.

Flat stock, such as basswood, is ideally suited to use as a simple trim for many dollhouse projects. It serves well because it provides the novice with an opportunity to become familiar and comfortable with trimming, and allows one to personally custom design the look of their house.

Flat stock is especially appropriate for Early American style homes. Back when the real homes were built, planing mills which could turn out fine trim and molding did not exist.

Once your house is "trimmed out," stand back and survey the craftsmanship! Look at the way in which the trim makes each room look truly finished. This was meant to be partly a learning experience, so take note of the visual effect of painted trim versus stained trim, and how each finish is appropriate for a particular setting. Once you feel comfortable as a dollhouse finisher, move on to tackle more complex and challenging projects. Other techniques of trim moldings that involve more intricate cuts and special installation techniques will be explained in future volumes.